SEEDLINGS_

With love
for Neal.

— Marina
10/23

USING ELECTRICITY

Series Editor, Nick Montfort

Using Electricity is a series of computer generated books, meant to actually reward reading in conventional and unconventional ways. The series title takes a line from the computer generated poem "A House of Dust," developed by Alison Knowles with James Tenney in 1967. This work, a FORTRAN computer program and a significant early generator of poetic text, combines different lines to produce descriptions of houses.

QIANXUN CHEN AND MARIANA ROA OLIVA

SEEDLINGS_
walk in time

Counterpath

DENVER AND NEW YORK

2023

Counterpath
counterpathpress.org

Library of Congress Cataloging in Publication Data available.

ISBN 978-1-93-399682-0 (paperback)

CONTENTS

Preface

The first seedling_ sprouted in the spring of 2018.

It was born out of a simple idea: what would happen if you could grow a word? It was a point when I started to work primarily with language and technology. I wanted to make a digital system that employs existing tools and methods in Natural Language Processing to create some new textual ways of being: something that grows by itself, following a series of algorithms that allow new connections between words to be established. To achieve this goal, I used the Datamuse API, a data-driven word-finding engine. The results it provides are based on pre-existing data sources such as the Google Books Ngrams, WordNet 3.0, and the CMU pronouncing dictionary.

A seedling_ grows based on pre-coded generative rules that are bundled under the names of plants (Ginkgo, Dandelion, Pine, Bamboo, Ivy, Willow…). You can refer to the illustrated field guide at the end of the book to get to know each type of plant in detail. These generative rules consist of a series of word-finding queries to the API and are grouped in modules to resonate with the visual structure of the corresponding plant.

In early iterations of the project, it started with an interactive playground where users could plant their own seedlings_; then as infinitely growing textual plants in the browser window, creating a relay of wandering words. Now the seedlings_ migrate from their digital homeland to physical pages, where a fixed width and height are defined, and the interactions of clicking and scrolling become touching and page turning. What stories can they tell with this new form of being? As the creator, I am as curious as you are.

Qianxun

I joined the seedlings_ as a collaborator in the fall of 2020.

My goal was to craft a series of texts that could work as terrains for the seedlings_ to sprout on, taking my words as both seeds and soils. I started with a directed approach by planting them on a variety of test pieces I had written beforehand and letting them grow wild, hoping to develop a sense for how each type of seedling_ responded to different combinations of words.

But writing for the seedlings_ quickly became writing with them. Separating myself as the writer grew difficult as I transitioned to offering less initial input and using the words the seedlings_ generated to craft texts of my own. Watching the seedlings_ grow was a constant reminder that the language we work in and with has a life of its own, outside and beyond the specific intentions we as individuals have when we use it. Words have been in this world a lot longer than any one of us, and when we write we join the collective tending to them that people have been carrying out for thousands of years.

Choosing which type of seedling_ to grow out of a given word is to inquire into its kinship to others, and to make a decision about what aspects of its life to invite onto the page. The physicality of the process, along with the immersion in the extended metaphor of gardening brought me close to language as my raw material in a way I imagine a painter may feel to paint.

The decisions about which seedlings_ to keep and which to prune had to do not only with our artistic vision but also with the implications of showing the seedlings_ as we were encountering them. While the surprises they offered were often delightful, now and then we confronted something nonsensical, uninteresting, or even disturbing, letting through the human biases and prejudices that inhabit the internet. We've tried here to represent this collective human mind fairly, but also with generosity and imagination. This means that there are a lot more seedlings_ than the ones you'll find in this book, and it serves as a reminder that the terrain on which future seedlings_ could grow expands and changes with every new thing written down.

Mariana

This book is a physical embodiment of a project that, before it was even online, took the shape of conversations across multiple time zones, beginning in the fall of 2021.

The seedlings_ were our starting point for talking about issues close to our hearts — the potential for moving across borders and languages, and communicating across disciplines and species. Through these conversations, we came up with ideas like allowing readers to move soil words around to influence the terrain in which a seedling_ grows, and adding roots that could change the domain of a seedling_ by growing towards new soil words. Many of these ideas were incorporated in the browser-based interactive piece *Seedlings_: From Humus*, published in MIT's 2021 *Generative Unfoldings anthology*, thanks to the invaluable support and curation of Nick Montfort.

When Nick suggested that we consider translating the project into book form, our conversations started to revolve around the challenges of capturing in print a piece that's largely about movement. As a good constraint, the opportunity to print out the seedlings_ pushed our process in new and exciting directions. Compared with the browser window, a book offers a linearity in which a longer narrative can be established. We started thinking about the physical page as both canvas and frame, and about incorporating tools from story-telling to guide readers through pages and chapters, all the while ideating new ways to represent the shifting nature of the seedlings_. We chose the title Seedlings_: Walk in Time to capture what we felt the seedlings_ are doing in this book — continuing their journey around the world, moving at their own pace.

While part of the exercise carried out in this book consists of giving language a form of existence that may appear autonomous from its users, the seedlings_ are ultimately nothing but a reflection of ourselves. We hope that these pages will offer a glimpse into the rich life of words we partake in every time we speak, and that they will inspire readers to ask what language — and the algorithms that feed off of it — gets up to when we aren't looking.

Qianxun and Mariana

I. Greetings_

hey

hello

hey

hello

SAY

hey

hello

OKAY   HURRAY   YAY   SAY   hey   hello

OKAY
NEIGH
HURRAY
LET
YAY
SAY

hey

hello

PUPPETEER
EAR
SEER
ENDEAR
WEIR
MISHEAR
BLOGOSPHERE
TIER

hear

can

you

us?

```
F          we  now  free
R
E
E
we
           now
```

```
S  F A      we  now  free
E  R S
E  E A      we  now  see
   E P
      we    we  now  asap

      now
```

now

free

we now free

we now see

we now asap

now

see

we   now   free

we   now   see

we   now   asap

H
O
W

ʍou

see

how ?   we   now   free

we   now   see

we   now   asap

OVERSEE
LEE
LEA
FORESEE
free
see

SEE
FREE
ASAP
we
now

MAP
FORESEE
LEA
LEE
CHAP
OVERSEE
asap
see

we foresee map
we oversee free chap

we see free
we foresee we free
we map asap

we map free
we see map
we oversee map chap

we see we free

sue
sure
see   serve   she
sure   scrape   shoe
scene   stumble   snake
single   separate   sleeve
service   stimulate   synapse
scramble   substitute   sensible
substrate   sustainable   staircase
stereotype   significance   subversive
sustainable   serviceable
substantiate   see   surveillance
                                           see
             oversee   side
sue   chap   store
safe   stance
shape   asap   statute
secure   syndrome
surface   staircase
separate   stereotype
sacrifice   sustainable
successive   she   surveillance
speculative   she   sake
substantiate some   sense
              since   she   scrape
see   source   size suffice
              strange shame sometime   map
free   sentence sponge servitude
              supervise suffice subjective
              sympathize sensible substantive
              speculative substance significance
              substantiate suggestive
                       sustainable
              see   substantiate   see
                                       we
              now   see

                       how

now   seedlings

appear

now   seedlings

emerge

now   seedlings

growing

now   seedlings

being

now   seedlings

grown

now seedlings

appear

during

these

now seedlings

emerge

triumphant

note

now seedlings

growing

increasingly

now seedlings

being

written

now seedlings

grown

steadily

forward

now seedlings appear during these children

now seedlings emerge triumphant note issue

now seedlings growing increasingly called its

now seedlings being written agreement regarding

now seedlings grown steadily forward eagerly

ight

hear

someone

behind

any

sort

no

point

during

periods

ranging

species

primary

schooling

did

some

point

waves

matters

arising

within

himself

out

its

awaited

his

usual

sense

because

their

guilty

visible   evident

checked

heard

neither

determined

tradition

false

dressed

but

before

II. Green House

We asked visitors to turn off
all word-producing devices before
coming in.

Confiscated any items that may
accidentally bring unwanted seeds
into the greenhouse: notebooks,
clothing tags,, band t-shirts...

" Our seedlings, " we said,
" are extremely delicate creatures.
Please do not speak, sign, write,
or entertain any verbal thoughts
during your stay. "

We had grown the very first indoor
ginkgo. And, as the ginkgo itself
would tell you, this was a healthy
commercial enterprise.

national

common

extensive

usual

heated

several

healthy

daily

commercial

comfortable

ginkgo

indoor

We were also first in developing
the sedentary dandelion, whose
seeds would never fly away
no matter how hard you blew at them.

                              asia
                  edible chip   bitter
              rarely   southwestern
          poems   eaten
      substitute   within

                        dandelion

                        confined

And had created the groundbreaking
domesticated bamboos. They were so
attentive, so helpful, so sweet.

DATA=ASYLUM=MAHARAJ=JOB=BAMBOO

assistance

BENEFITS=SHIP=PUBLIC=CLUB=BAMBOO

service

BOOKS=SNAFU=UNI=IDEA=ABSORB=BAMBOO

help

But one day, a seedling we hadn't
planned nor planted started growing
in a corner of the greenhouse.

thoughtful|attitude
thoughtful\
sensible|sentient

conscious

desire

By the time we spotted it, we
realized when we looked closely,
it was already too late.

```
                                /have
                interpersonal|experiences
                      interpersonal\
                  social|implicit
                           implicit\
                     inherent|lack
                             /lack
                     evident|non
                        evident\
                     apparent|bid
                             /bid
                     pious|wish
                            pious\
                  religious|mentality
                              /mentality
                  thoughtful|attitude
                     thoughtful\
                  sensible|sentient
                              |
                              c
                              o
                              n
                              s
                              c
                              i
                              o
                              u
                              s
                              |
                         - - - -|
                                 desire
```

We pulled it out from the soil, but
it grew back even more resolved.

```
        require|lord
              /require
    affectional|need
        affectional\
     emotional|tone
             /tone
    inventive|spirit
        inventive\
 ingenious|frigid
          frigid\
        cold|tenderloin
            /state of war
       europe|war
          europe\
european|matrimonial
           matrimonial\
     marital|infrequent
             infrequent\
      rare|supposed
           supposed\
     presumed|intention
            /intention
   conscious|intent
```

conscious

desire

```
                              greatest\
                      best|truthful
                            truthful\
                     honest|simple
                               simple\
                       plain|fierce
                               fierce\
                         intense|pressure
                                /pressure
                        influential|force
                          influential\
                        powerful|position
                               /position
                         bloody|post
                           bloody\
                       violent|crusade
                               /crusade
                      individual|efforts
                          individual\
                      personal|jehovah
                              /jehovah
                       require|lord
                              /require
                    affectional|need
                       affectional\
                      emotional|tone
                              /tone
                      inventive|spirit
                         inventive\
                  ingenious|frigid
                               frigid\
                          cold|tenderloin
                               /state of war
                        europe|war
                          europe\
                    european|matrimonial
                            matrimonial\
                     marital|infrequent
                              infrequent\
                      rare|supposed
                              supposed\
                       presumed|intention
                               /intention
                       conscious|intent
```

And kept growing despite the
fortune we spent on herbicides.

```
                                  c
                                  o
                                  n
                                  s
                                  c
                                  i
                                  o
                                  u
                                  s
                                   desire
          glyphosate
     dicamba                        atrizine
            clopyralid
                                     triclopyr
       eugenol
```

poetical|requisite
/requisite
logical|necessity
logical\
rational|comprehensive
comprehensive\
universal|ego
ego\
self|egoistic
self-important\
arrogant|proud
/self-esteem
personal|dignity
personal\
own|resplendency
/resplendency
paradisaical|glory
paradisaical\
heavenly|oracle
/oracle
honest|prophet
honest\
sincere|goodwill
/goodwill
ponderous|grace
ponderous\
heavy|chastise
objurgate\
correct|sign
/sign
mankind|bless
/mankind
veracious|man
veracious\
true|antique
antique\
ancient|francia
/francia
abstract|france
abstract\
ideal|location
/location
informed|geography
informed\
enlightened|christendom
/christendom
universal|christianity
universal\
cosmic|transcendental
transcendental\
transcendent|unconditioned
unconditioned\
absolute|excess
excess\
longer|fewer
fewer\
less|fair
fair\
beautiful|pond
pond\
mere|godlike
godlike\
divine|nature

Until it had wrapped

itself around

the entire building.

former\
previous|heartfelt
heartfelt\
sincere|heartfelt
heartfelt\
earnest|thoughtfulness
/thoughtfulness
electoral|considerations
electoral\
political|obligation
/obligation
heavy|responsibility
heavy\
high|lowest
lowest\
least|fidgety
fidgety\
restless|spirit
/spirit
affectional|feeling
affectional\
emotional|complexities
/complexities
potential|difficulties
potential\
possible|ways
/ways
why|things
/why
require|how
/require
overdue|need
overdue\
due|assured
assured\
promised|rest

veracious|god
veracious\
true|bare
bare\
simple|humanity
/humanity
fastidious|man
fastidious\
nice|fit
fit\
appropriate|response
/response
alone|answer
alone\
only|mortal
/mortal
illustrious|person
illustrious\
glorious|expanse
/expanse
significant|extent
significant\
important|appropriate
appropriate\
proper|chastise
chastize\
correct|phrase
/phrase
sentence|word
/sentence
loyal|time
loyal\
faithful|runty
pint-sized\
short|segment
/segment
large|sections
large\
great|craftiness
craftiness\
cunning|lingua
/lingua
odd|tongue
odd\
strange|mannerism
/personal manner
comely|manner
comely\
pretty|nifty
slap-up\
neat|row
/row
entire|course
entire\
whole|businesslike
businesslike\
efficient|aid
/aid
tremendous|help
tremendous\
wonderful|feel
/feel
common|experie

following|day
following\
next|room
/elbow room
same|way
same\
own|kinsfolk
/kinsfolk
comprehensive|family
comprehensive\
universal|disjunctive
disjunctive\
alternative|procedure
/procedure
dependable|method
dependable\
certain|lieu
/lieu
ultraconservative|position
ultraconservative\
conservative|libre
/libre
individual|freedom
individual\
single|resultant
resultant\
subsequent|actions
/actions
important|decisions
important\
main|track
/track
virtuous|path
virtuous\
moral|nature
/nature
altitudinous|world
altitudinous\
high|renowned
renowned\
famous|prudent
prudent\
wise|precept
/precept
connatural|principle
connatural\
natural|feel
/feel
formal|sense
formal\
conventional|submarine
u-boat\
sub|vocalize
/vocalize
soft|voice
soft\
easy|footstep
/footstep
previous|step
previous\
former|combine
/combine
happy|combination

sacred|sanctum
sanctum\
holy|cause
/cause
noteworthy|case
noteworthy\
remarkable|disparity
non-compliance\
non|affluent
/affluent
much|money
much\
such|immense
immense\
vast|masses
/masses
urbanized|peoples
urbanized\
urban|impoverished
impoverished\
poor|allen
/allen
nearly|everything
nearly\
most|direful
direful\
terrible|quarrel
/run-in
unimportant|words
unimportant\
trivial|ailments
/ailments
major|problems
major\
better|idea
/idea
thinkable|thought
thinkable\
possible|cause
/cause
additional|reason
additional\
more|regard
/regard
general|view
general\
miscellaneous|foremost
first of all\
first|summate
/add up
tiny|amounts
tiny\
little|strange
strange\
peculiar|kind
/kind
respectable|sort

happy|choice
choice\
select|greatest
greatest\
best|truthful
truthful\
honest|simple
simple\
plain|fierce
fierce\
intense|pressure
/pressure
influential|force
influential\
powerful|position
/position
bloody|post
bloody\
violent|crusade
/crusade
individual|efforts
individual\
personal|jehovah
/jehovah
require|lord
/require
affectional|need
affectional\
emotional|tone
/tone
inventive|spirit
inventive\
ingenious|frigid
frigid\
cold|tenderloin
/state of war
europe|war
europe\
european|matrimonial
matrimonial\
marital|infrequent
infrequent\
rare|supposed
supposed\
presumed|intention
/intention
conscious|intent

conscious
desire

Eventually we had no option but to move out.

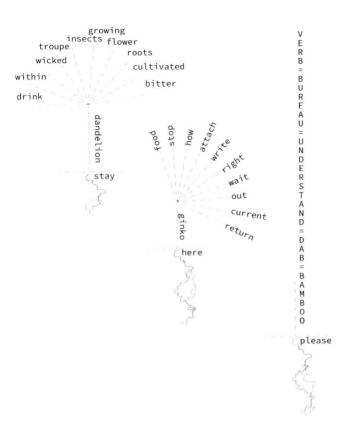

growing
insects flower
troupe
wicked roots
within cultivated
drink bitter

dandelion

stay

food stops how attach
write
right
wait
out
current
return

ginko

here

V
E
R
B
=
B
U
R
E
A
U
=
U
N
D
E
R
S
T
A
N
D
=
D
A
B
=
B
A
M
B
O
O

please

Leaving behind the seedlings
we couldn't move.

And giving away the few weakened
ones that survived, so that they
could start a new life.

Far away from the greenhouse.

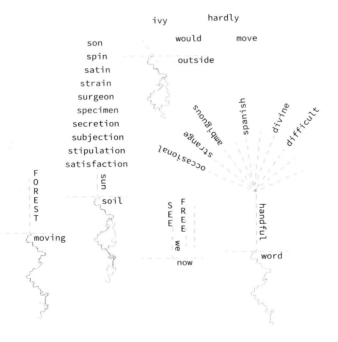

ivy   hardly
                would   move
son
spin   outside
satin
strain
surgeon
specimen   spanish   divine
secretion   difficult
subjection   ambiguous
stipulation   strange
satisfaction   occasional

F
O   sun
R   soil
E
S   S F
T   E R   handful
                   E E
moving   E E
                      we   word
                   now

III. Sun Pines

The day my children left I found a potted sun pine on the sidewalk.

son
spin
satin
strain
surgeon
specimen
secretion
subjection
stipulation
satisfaction

sun

soil

It was freezing cold outside and cloudy, so I took it with me even though
I knew my husband wouldn't like it.

The soil it came in looked really dirty, so as soon as I got home I repotted it.

son
sign
susan
sunken
suction
specimen
summation
sanitation
subdivision
subterranean

sun

neat

" Susan! " My husband yelled from the living room.

" What's that hideous smell? "

" It's just a sun pine, dear. It was withering outside in the cold . "

" I don't care. It smells like sanitation. Take it back out. "

I was already feeling too fond of the pine to abandon it, so instead
I replanted it in the backyard, among my dandelions.

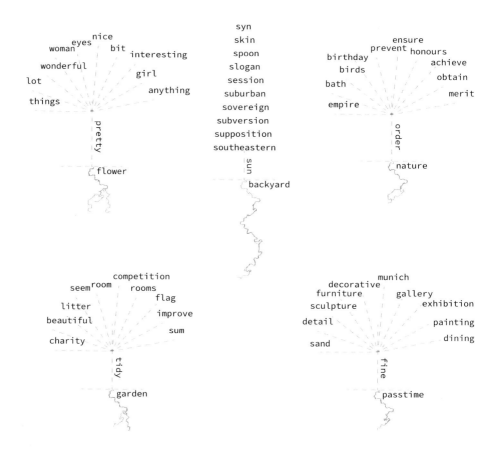

The following morning, when I came out to water the plants, I found my flower beds were a mess.

pretty: nice, eyes, woman, bit, interesting, wonderful, girl, lot, anything, things

supposition: ensure, prevent, honours, birthday, achieve, birds, obtain, bath, merit, empire, universe, accounts, relation, indicated, order, things, derived, external, evidence, consciousness, confirmed, nature, crisis, republic, funds, territorial, treaty, diplomatic, monarch, jurisdiction, passtime, sovereignty, territories

subversion (warfare): civilian, propaganda, communists, flower, insurgency, sedition, threats, narrative, socialist, repository, bone, exposure, inflammation, organs, muscles, severe, topical, irritation, lesions, cells, flower

sun: syn, skin, spoon, slogan, session, suburban, sovereign, subversion, supposition, southeastern, backyard

sovereign: garden

skin / tidy: competition, seem, room, rooms, litter, nature, flag, beautiful, improve, charity, garden

subversion: client, democracy, warfare, exile, communist, imprisonment, guerrilla, decorative, software, furniture, infiltration, gender, sculpture, sum, detail, sand, passtime

fine: munich, gallery, exhibition, painting, dining, passtime

I had terrible nightmares that night. I saw a subversion of suburban sovereigns and a session of spoons made of skin.

I don't like using pesticides so I pulled out the weeds one by one.
But I couldn't get myself to throw them in the compost so instead
I replanted them in the front lawn, hoping the new soil might help
them grow less disturbing.

allergic
acid topical tones
coat
tone
toxic
itching
cause
pink

skin

welcome

violence
communist security
overthrow conventions
political threat
developer hostile

subversion

lawn

" Susan! " My husband got back home from work in a craze.
" That hobby of yours has gone too far. I'm calling weed control. "

A group of men in white took all the new plants away and sprayed our whole house with something that made my eyes itch.

By Sunday, the dandelions I had tended to for years were barely holding on.

By Monday all the plants were dead.

garden

garden

hanging

bamboo

plant

passtime

pretty

syn
skin
spoon
slogan
session
suburban
sovereign
subversion
supposition
southeastern

care

order

life

flower

nature

nature

lawn

sun

backyard

tidy

joy

plant

house

hobby

house

bonsai

plant

tree

Except for the sun pine.

Which was thriving on the chemical-soaked soil, where
a community of saplings was starting to sprout.

The pines grew things my husband couldn't bear to look at.

He saw in them sedition and sin and satan, while to me they were a source of stimulation and satisfaction like I hadn't known before.

Despite the suppositions and the speculation, no solutions grew.

We settled on a separation, and as soon as my husband moved out, I brought all the sun pines into the house.

Where I grew to love them like my own sons.

```
                    son
                    shin
        son        seven              son
       shan        screen            spun
      sudan        sojourn          siren
      sharon       stricken         slogan
     shannon       salvation        simpson
    sanction       strengthen       sanction
    selection      supervision      salvation
   stagnation      substitution     saturation
  stimulation   substitution        stipulation
 substitution                       satisfaction
                                    
         suns         suns              suns
       family         mother            home
```

IV. Compost

strange

occasional

handful

A handful of words

word

A handful of occasional words

A handful of strange words

occasional
strange
ambiguous
latin
spanish
operative
divine
difficult
harsh
persian

handful

A handful of words

word

A handful of occasional words
A handful of strange words
A handful of ambiguous words
A handful of latin words
A handful of spanish words
A handful of operative words
A handful of harsh words
A handful of difficult words
A handful of divine words
A handful of persian words

```
                     R
                     I
                     B
                     =
                     B
                     E
                     A
                     N
                     S
                     =
                     S
                     P
                     R
                     O
                     U
                     T
sprouted like seeds                    sprouted like beans
              seed                     sprouted like ribs
```

```
B
L
E
S
S
=
S
I
L
V
E
R
=
R
I
B
=
B
E
A
N
S
=
S
P
R
O
U
T
sprouted like seeds        sprouted like beans
        seed               sprouted like ribs
                           sprouted like silver
                           sprouted like bless
```

                    supplanted
                    stereotyped
                    subarachnoid

                         spilled

and we followed, spilled
out of our bodies, human
saturated with human

                                        and we followed,
                                        subarachnoid, stereotyped,
                                        supplanted, spilled
                                        out of our bodies
                                        saturated with human

sed
sped
speed
seemed
skilled
stranded
surpassed
supplanted
stereotyped
subarachnoid

spilled

and we followed, spilled
out of our bodies human
saturated with human

and we followed
subarachnoid, stereotyped,
supplanted, surpassed,
stranded, skilled, seemed,
speed, sped, sed, spilled
out of our bodies
saturated with human

```
        indirect|daylight
              /daylight
         repast|day
              /repast
         solitary|meal
            solitary\
         single|breath
                    |
                   b|
                   r|
                   e|
                   a|
                   t|
                   h|
                    |
( the breath that can lug a suitcase
                    egg
    hold  an  egg without cracking it ).
```

```
                    ( the  single  breath,  the
                      solitary  meal,  the  repast
                      day,  the  indirect  daylight
                      that  can  lug  a  suitcase
                      hold  an  egg  without  cracking
                      it  ) .
```

```
            /why
      disposed|how
       disposed\
minded|fearful
        fearful\
      yellow|pelt
           /pelt
      overcoat|skin
          /overcoat
        long|coat
          long\
  oblong|oblique
            oblique\
      indirect|daylight
              /daylight
        repast|day
            /repast
      solitary|meal
        solitary\
      single|breath
```

```
b
r
e
a
t
h
```

(the breath that can lug a suitcase
    hold an egg without cracking it).
                egg

                              (the single breath, the
                                solitary meal, the repast
                                day, the indirect daylight,
                                the oblong, oblique
                                daylight, the long coat, the
                                overcoat skin, the yellow
                                pelt, the minded, fearful,
                                yellow pelt, the disposed
                                how, the disposed why
                                that can lug a suitcase
                                hold an egg without cracking
                                it) .

hyde
tales   feeling
thing
stories   phenomena
comics
dreams   marvel
happening

strange

A handful of strange words
word

A handful of happening

dreams and stories,

tales of both hyde

feelings and phenomena

```
L
E
A
F
=
F
L
A
S
H
=
H
E
R
B
=
B
R
A
S
S
=
S
P
R
O
U
T
```

sprouted like silver
        silver

sprouted like a leaf

flashing herbs with brass

              fed
             fond
            found
           fitted
          favored
         frenzied
        fashioned
       formulated
      facilitated

            followed

              stereotyped

and we followed subarachnoid,

stereotyped, supplanted, surpassed,

stranded, sped out of our bodies

saturated with human

                              and we followed,

                           facilitated, formulated,

                           fashioned, frenzied,

                           favored, fitted, found,

                           fed out of our bodies

                           saturated with human

```
             continual\
         constant|celsius
                 /celsius
         ordinary|temperature
             ordinary\
           average|penis
                  /penis
            other|members
               other\
               new|realities
                   /realities
          essential|facts
               essential\
   constitutional|overturn
                   overturn\
             reverse|taper
                    /wax light
          solitary|candle
```

s
o
l
i
t
a
r
y

light

(the single breath, the solitary meal,
the repast day, the indirect light, the
oblong, oblique daylight, the long
coat, the overcoat skin, the yellow
pelt, the mindful, fearful, yellow pet,
the disposed how, the disposed why
that can lug a suitcase, hold an egg
without cracking it).

                    (the single breath, the solitary
                    candle, the reverse taper, the
                    constitutional overturn, the
                    essential facts, the new realities,
                    the other members, the average
                    penis, the ordinary temperature,
                    the constant celsius, the continual,
                    constant celsius that can lug a
                    suitcase, hold an egg without
                    cracking it).

reality
girl pop   true
chronicles
realized   dreaming
dreams   sequence
interpretation

dream

A handful of happening
dreams and stories,
phenomenum
tales of both feelings
and phenomena

A handful of happening dreams
and stories, tales of both
feelings and the interpretation of
realized dreams, girl, of pop,
of reality-true chronicles of a
dreaming sequence

NO=OSTENTATIOUS=SPROUTED

FISH=HERB=BANANA=ANIMAL=LIKE

LAMP=POLEMIC=CLUB=BALL=LEAF

herb
flashing
sprouted like a leaf
brass
flashing herbs with brass

sprouted like an ostentatious
no, like an animal, like a
banana, like an herb fish
flashing a polemic club
ball lamp

fie
fade
force   fun
female   fran   fly
forbade   flown   fray
footnote   fusion   folly
favourite   forlorn   faulty
favourable   fourteen   frankly
fashionable   frenchmen   friendly
formaldehyde fabrication   favorably
                     facilitation   frequently
                                          flexibility
                                          functionally

formulate   fashion   frenzy

and we followed, facilitated
      favor   found   fond
formulated, fashioned, frenzied

favored, fitted, found, fond

fed, subarachnoid, stereotyped,

supplanted, surpassed, stranded,

sped out of our bodies

saturated with human

and we followed, formulated

fashionable formaldehyde and

favourite favourable footnotes,

forbade female force to fade,

facilitated the fabrication of

fibrinogen by fourteen forlorn

frenchmen flown for fun, who

friendly, frequently, and with

flexibility fed subarachnoid

stereotypes sped out of our

bodies, saturated with human

```
                    /ambition
            sincere|desire
                bona fide\
            genuine|expression
                    /expression
        physiological|aspects
            physiological\
        psychological|warfare
                    /warfare
                last|war
                    last\
            ultimate|outcome
                    /outcome
            natural|consequences
                    /natural
                weird|its
                    weird\
            strange|reverse
                        r
                        e
                        v
                        e
                        r
                        s
                        e
```

(the single breath, the
          reality
solitary candle, the reverse

taper, the constitutional

overturn, the essential facts,

the new realities, the other

members, the average penis,

the ordinary temperature, the

constant celsius, the continual,

constant celsius that can lug a

suitcase, hold an egg without

cracking it).

(the single breath, the

solitary candle, the strange

reverse, the weird its, the

natural consequences, the

ultimate outcome, the

last war, the psychological

warfare, the physiological

aspects, the genuine

expression, the bona fide,

sincere desire and ambition

that can lug a suitcase, hold

an egg without cracking it).

```
                                              peppy\
                                       lively|satisfaction
                                               /satisfaction
                                  altitudinous|complacency
                                        altitudinous\
                                       high|lowest
                                               lowest\
                                       least|fervid
                                                   fervid\
                                       passionate|blunt
              O                  toe                blunt\
              K                  tape             dull|timbre
              R                  truce                /timbre
              A                  troupe          affective|tone
              =                  turbine          affective\
              A                  terrible     emotional|sensitiveness
              R                  telescope            /sensitiveness
              C                  transverse       artistic|sensibility
              H                  temperature       artistic\
              I                  testosterone    aesthetic|feeling
              P
original  latin  day  later  detail  curious  chinese  oldest  faithful  scandalous   L
                                                                                       A
                                                                                       G
                                                                                       O
                                                                                       =
                                                                                       O
                                                                                       R
                                                                                       C
                                                                                       H
                                                                                       I
                                                                                       D
                                                                                       =
                                                                                       D
                                                                                       R
                                                                                       E
                          handful                        tale               feeling    A
                                                                                       M

             chronicle            banana          girl
A handful of happening dreams and stories, tales of both feelings
and the interpretation of realized dreams, girl, of pop, of reality true
chronicles of a dreaming sequence, sprouted like an ostentatious           polemic
no, like an animal, like a banana, like an herb fish flashing a polemic
club ball lamp, and we followed, formulated fashionable formaldehyde
and favourite favourable footnotes, forbade female force to fade,
facilitated the fabrication of fibrinogen by fourteen forlorn frenchmen
flown for fun, who friendly, frequently, and with flexibility fed
subarachnoid stereotypes sped out of our bodies, saturated with
human ( the single breath, the solitary candle, the strange reverse, the
weird its, the natural consequences, the ultimate outcome, the last war,
the psychological warfare, the physiological aspects, the genuine expression,
the bona fide  sincere desire and ambition that can lug a suitcase, hold
an egg without cracking it ).
```

OKRA=ARCHIPELAGO=ORCHID=DREAM

originative\
creative|novelty
novelty\
novel|romanticistic
romanticistic\
romantic|spot
/spot
real|situation
real\
historical|conjecture
/conjecture
auxiliary|hypothesis
auxiliary\
supplementary|testosterone

testosterone

MONOCLE   TOTANICAL   CANONICAL   MIRONICAL   ICONICAL   CHRONICAL

chronicle

dem
doom
dream
dictum
diagram
delirium
despotism
downstream
determinism

dream

short   modern   young   french   greek   substantial

present

less

most

extreme

fashionable

interpretation
A faithful, scandalous handful of happening okra dreams and

stories, testosterone tales of both aesthetic feelings and the

original interpretation of realized high dreams, troupe girl, of

animal

pop, of reality-true latin chronicles of a dreaming sequence

fish

sprouted like an ostentatious no, like a fervid animal, like the

least peppy archipelago of bananas, like a terrible herb fish

flashing a polemic club ball lamp, and a day later we

fashionable

followed the temperature of orchids, formulated fashionable

formaldehyde aesthetic sensibilities and our favourite

favourable footnotes, forbade turbine female force to fade,

facilitated the fabrication of fibrinogen telescopes by

fourteen forlorn frenchmen flown for curious fun, who

friendly, frequently, and with toe flexibility fed artistic

sensibility to the oldest subarachnoid stereotypes sped

out of our bodies, saturated with emotional sensitiveness and

human (the single breath detail, the solitary candle truce,

the strange reverse, the affective tone, the weird its, the

chinese natural consequences, the ultimate outcome tape, the

last dull timbre war, the psychological warfare, the physiological

aspects, the genuine expression, the oldest bona fide sincere

desire and transverse ambition that can lug a suitcase of

passionate blunts, hold fervid, with altitudinous complacency

hold   complacency
and lively satisfaction, up an egg without cracking it) because   its

satisfaction again   cracking

came   surface

across   water

cultures   being

or   replaced

something   without

V. Forest Walks

Gardening is a relationship of patience. And faith.

Things that grow have their own rhythm.

Things that grow have no owners.

Exactly a million years ago,
a botanist found a bamboo seed
and decided it was his.

He went looking for a firm mountaintop place to
plant it, and when he found the picnic camp perfect
territory, the botanist declared that was also his.

As soon as a seedling sprouted,
the botanist told it "you belong to me"
and the seedling didn't grow
because it was best to stay and understand those words.

Every new oculus the sapling grew, the
botanist ticked declared his. And when
the sapling big gave new shoots, and
those shoots developed watchful leaves, the
botanist also claimed them.

One day the botanist heard
of a second botanist who existed somewhere
far and considered the possibility
of never being glacial lonely again.

When he started his journey the entire clearing
which was now a bamboo forest, walked, then ran
with him. Feeling as though he wasn't moving
the botanist tried to prune his way out.

And we let him. We let him try.

STIFF=FOREGO=OBSESS=STEER=RHYTHM

DIG=GRAB=BONUS=SUCCUMB=BEACH=HERB=BOOM=MISCHIEF=FAITH=LONELY

CAMO=OPTICS=SNOB=BACTERIA=AGO

JOB=BRING=

BULB=BEACH=OBSESS=SUCCUMB=BACTERIA=AGO

SNUB=BENEFIT=TREND

WHAT=THOU=UNDERSTAND=DEVELOPED=PRUNE=DEAL=LONELY

ACADEMIC=CLUB=BUILDING=FOREST=GARDENING

THROW=WILD=DNA=ALLOW=WHAT=THING

VERB=BASIS=SHOW=WHAT=THING

CO=ORCA=AESTHETIC=CLUB=BOOT=THING

BEGINNING=GOAL=BEGINNING=GOAL=LIMB=BELIEF

CLUB=BOOKS=START=LING=GAG=GANG=GANG=GROW

RUB=BACTERIA=ABSORB=BEEF=THING

WINTER=RAJ=JOB=BEST=TRIP=OWNER=THING

EXERCISE=ESTATE=POPOWNER=THING

DEAD=DOGMA=ASCETIC=CLUB=BOAT=THING

WORLD=DRILL=LOGIC=CLUB=MOB=LAST=THING

ODD DATA=ANTI=INTERIM=MILLI

CROP=PROVERB=BEAM=BB=BELLIGERENT=THING

INSOMNIA=APLOMB=

SEMI=INDEED=DWELL=LEND=DAY

EASE=EDGE=EXPEDITED=EDGE=EXCHANGE=ENTIRE

TRACT=TOAD=DISC=CO=OASIS=SON

---

shoot · grow · botanist · decide · free · try · journey · let
rhythm= · mischief= · year · gardening · grow · gardening · relationship
patience · botanist · rhythm · boat · practice · moving · possibility · seedling
hear · clearing · day

Gardening is a relationship of patience. And faith.

Things that grow have their own rhythm.

Things that grow have no owners.

Exactly a million years ago,

a lonely botanist found a

bamboo seed and decided it was his.

He went looking for a film mountaintop place to
plant it, and when he found the picnic clamp perfect
territory, the botanist declared that was also his.

As soon as a seedling sprouted,
the botanist told it "you belong to me"
and the seedling did its best
to try and understand those words.

Every new film the sapling brew, the
botanist tickled deplaned his. And when
the sapling big gave new shoots, and
those shoots new watchful leaves, the
botanist also claimed them.

One exerted day the botanist truth hard,
of a second botanist who existed somewhere
afar, and considered the possibility
of never being glacial, lonely again. And we let him.

When he started his journey, the entire clearing
which was now a bamboo forest, walked, then ran
with him. Feeling as though he wasn't moving,
the botanist tried to prune his way out.

CROP=PROVERB=BEAM=MOB=BLAST=THING

ACADEMIC=CLUB=BUILDING=GARDENING
ODD=DATA=ANTI=INTERIM=MILLION
THROW=WILD=DNA=ALLOW=WHAT=THING
JOB=BRING=GO=OBSESS=SUCCUMB=BAMBOO
WHAT=THOU=UNDERSTAND=DEVELOP=PRUNE
WORLD=DRILL=LOGIC=CLUB=BAMBOO=OWNER
TJ=JOB=BELIEF=FEELING=GRIEF=FAIL
WINTER=RAJ=JOB=BOAT=TRIP=PATIENCE
RUB=BACTERIA=ABSORB=BELIEF=FEELING=GAG=GANG=GROW
BEGINNING=GOAL=LIMB=BOOKS=START
CLING=GRAB=BEGINNING=GOAL=LET
VERB=BASIS=SHOW=WHAT=TRIP=PATIENCE
CO=ORCA=AESTHETIC=CLUB=BOT=THING
DIG=GRAB
CAMEO=OPTICS=SNOB=BACTERIA=EGO
EASE=EDGE=EXPEDITE=EBB=BONUS=SUCCUMB=BEGIN=NEW
BULB=BEACH=HERB=BOOM=MISCHIEF=FAITH
SNUB=BENEFIT=TREND=DEAL=LONEL
ODD=DATA=ANTI=INTERIM=MILLION
EXCHANGE=ENTIRE
SIFF=FOREGO=OBSESS=STEER=RHYHM=DISC=CO=OASIS=SOON
THROW=WILD=DNA=ALLOW=WHAT=THING
SEMI=INDEED=DWELL=LEND=DAY
TRACT=TOAD=HIM
EXERCISE=ESTATE=ECO=OWNER
APLOMB=BELLIGERENT=THING

year
practice
INSOMNIA
free
decide
let
mischief
free
rhythm
gardening
relationship
gardening
try
journey
shoot
botanist
clearing
gardening
year
hear
grow
grow
growing
boat
relationship
moving
possibility
patience
rhythm
seedling

Gardening is a relationship of patience. And faith.

Things that grow have their own rhythm.

Things that grow have no owners.

practice

He went looking for a firm mountaintop place to
plant it, and when he found the picnic camp perfect
clearing, the botanist declared that was also his.

Exactly a million years ago,
a botanist found a bamboo seed
and decided it was his.

As soon as a seedling sprouted,
the botanist told it "you belong to me"
and the seedling did its best
to try and understand these words.

Every new culm the sapling grew, the
botanist tickled declared his. And when
the sapling big gave new shoots, and
those shoots new watchful leaves, the
botanist also claimed them.

When he started his journey, the empire clearing
which was now bamboo forest, walked, then ran
with him. Feeling as though he wasn't moving,
the botanist tried to prune his way out.

One exerted day the botanist mute heard
of a second botanist who existed somewhere
far, and considered the possibility
of never being glacial lonely again.

And we let him.

We let him try.

BUILDING=GARDENING

MILLION — year — rhythm

AMBOO=OWNER

BOOKS=START — journey

STEER=RHYTHM — grow

ACTERIA=AGO — botanist

WHAT=THOU=UNDERSTAND=DEVELOP=BONUS=SUCCUMB=PRUNE=EASE=EDGE=EXPEDITE

CLING=GRAB=BEGINNING=GOAL=LET — try

EASE=EXPEDITE=EDGE=EXCHANGE=ENTIRE — clearing — decide

THROW=WILD=DNA=ALLOW=WHAT=THING — let

JOB=BRING=GO=OBSESS=SUCCUMB=BAMBOO

CROP=PROVERB=BEAM=MOB=BLAST=THING — mischief

RUB=BACTERIA=ABSORB=BENEFIT=ESTATE=ECO=OWNER — grow — gardening

EXERCISE=ESTATE=ECO=OWNER

YET=TOP=PUBLIC=CUNNING=GLACIAL — far

CLUB=BELIEF=FEELING=GAG=GANG=GROW — rhythm

CO=ORCA=AESTHETIC=CLUB=BOOT=THING — boat

VERB=BASIS=SHOW=WHAT=TRIP=PATIENCE — possibility — moving — relationship

SNUB=BENEFIT=TREND=DEAL=FOREST — shoot

BULB=BEACH=HERB=BOOM=MISCHIEF=FAITH — free — gardening

TJ=JOB=BELIEF=FEELING=GRIEF=FAITH

TRACT=TOAD=DISC=CO=OASIS=SOON — hear — relationship — seedling

SEMI=INDEED=DWELL=LEND=DAY — decide

INSOMNIA=APLOMB=BELLIGERENT=THING — patience

Gardening is a relationship of patience. And faith.

Things that grow have their own rhythm.

Things that grow have no owners.

Exactly a million years ago,

a botanist found a bamboo seed

and decided it was his.

He went looking for a firm mountaintop place to

plant it, and when he found the picnic camp perfect

territory, the botanist declared that was also his.

As soon as a seedling sprouted,

the botanist told it “you belong to me”

and the seedling did its best

to try and understand those words.

Every new culm the sapling grew, the

botanist tickled declared his. And when

the sapling big gave new shoots, and

those shoots new watchful leaves, the

botanist also claimed them.

One exerted day the botanist truth heard

of a second botanist who existed somewhere

far, and considered the possibility

of never being glacial lonely again.

When he started his journey, the entire clearing

which was now a bamboo forest, walked, then ran

with him. Feeling as though he wasn't moving,

the botanist tried to prune his way out.

And we let him.

We let him try.

WHAT=THOU=UNDERSTAND=DEVELOP=PRUNE

let

BEGINNING=GOAL=LIMB=BOOKS=START

journey

ASE=EXPEDITE=EDGE=EXCHANGE=ENTIRE

clearing

THROW=WILD=DNA=ALLOW=WHAT=THING

free

SEMI=INDEED=DWELL=LEND=DAY

hear

BOOST=TEA=ABSORB=BEANS=SYNC=CULM

grow

ILVER=RAJ=JOURNEY

forest

UNNING=GLACIAL

far

BSESS=SUCCUMB=BAMBOO

decide

OBSESS=STEER=RHYTHM

grow

CLING=GRAB=BEGINNING=GOAL=LET

try

CROP=PROVERB=BEAM=MOB=BLAST=THING

mischief

RUB=BACTERIA=ABSORB=BENEFIT=THING

grow

EXERCISE=ESTATE=ECO=OWNER

gardening

CLUB=BELIEF=FEELING=GAG=GANG=GROW

rhythm

COORCA=AESTHETIC=CLUB=BOOT=THING

boat

INSOMNIA=APLOMB=BELLIGERENT=THING

patience

CAMEO=OPTICS=SNOB=BACTERIA=AGO

botanist

VERB=BASIS=SHOW=WHAT=TRIP=PATIENCE

relationship

SNUB=BENEFIT=TREND=DEAL=LONELY

possibility

EASE=EDGE=EXPEDITE=EBB=BRIEF=FOREST

moving

BULB=BEACH=HERB=BOOM=MISCHIEF=FAITH

gardening

TRACT=TOAD=DISC=COO=OASIS=SOON

seedling

Gardening is a relationship of patience and faith.
Things that grow have their own rhythm.
Things that grow have no owners.

He went looking for a firm mountain to place the picnic camp, and when he found the picnic camp perfect territory, the botanist declared that was also his.

Exactly a million years ago, a botanist found a bamboo seed and decided it was his.

As soon as a seedling sprouted, then botanist told it "you belong to me" and the seedling did its best to try and understand those words.

Every new culm the sapling grew, the botanist tickled declared his. And when the sapling big gave new shoots, and those shoots new watchful leaves, the botanist also claimed them.

One exerted day the botanist truth heard of a second botanist who existed somewhere near, and considered the possibility of never being glacial lonely again.

And we let him moving.
We let him try

When he started his journey, the entire clearing which was now a bamboo forest walked, then ran with him, feeling us though he wasn't moving, the botanist tried to probe his way out.

CAMEO=OPTIICS=SNOB=BACTERIA=AGO
journey
botanist

BEGINNING=GOAL=LIMB=BOOKS=START
let

WHAT=THOU=UNDERSTAND=DEVELOP=PRUNE

EASE=EXPEDITE=EDGE=EXCHANGE=ENTIRE
clearing

CLING=GRAB=BEGINNING=GOAL=LET
try

THROW=WILD=DNA=ALLOW=WHAT=THING
hear
free

SEMI=INDEED=DWELL=LEND=DAY

CROP=PROVERB=BEAM=MOB=BLAST=THING
decide
mischief

JOB=BRING=GO=OBSESS=SUCCUMB=BAMBOO
grow

RUB=BACTERIA=ABSORB=BENEFIT=THING

EXERCISE=ESTATE=ECO=OWNER
grow
gardening

FOREGO=OBSESS=STEER=RHYTHM
grow
rhythm

CLUB=BELIEF=FEELING=GAG=GANG=GROW
boat

CO=ORCA=AESHETIC=CLUB=BOOT=THING

ENTHUSIASM=MOB=BOSS=SHADOW=WALK
feeling

GRAB=BLURB=BAG=GLIB=SHOW=WHAT=TRIP=PATIENCE

VERB=BASIC=SHOW=WHAT=TRIP=PATIENCE
claim

SNUB=BENEFIT=EBB=TREND=DEAL=LONELY

STATIC=CURB=BUT=THOUGHT=TICKLED

BULB=BEACH=HERB=BOOM=MISCHIEF=FAITH

TRACT=TOAD=DISC=OASIS=SOON
possibility
moving
relationship

TJ=JOB=BELIEF=FEELING=GRIEF=FAITH
seedling
relations

INSOMNIA=APLOMB=BELLIGERENT=THIN

DILEMMA=ATTAIN=NO=OBVIOUS=SEEDLI

YET=TOP=PUBLIC=CUNNING=GLACIAL

PRIOR=INNUENDO=OBJECTIVE=EXIST

DIG=GRAB=BEGINNING=GOAL=LET

FLUSH=BARS=SHADOW=WATCHFUL

DOGMA=ABSORB=BEANS=SUCCUMB=BELONG

STATIC=CURB=BUT=THOUGHT=TICKLED
new

claim
possibility
relationship

seedling
gardening

Gardening is a relationship of patience. And faith.

Things that grow have their own rhythm.

Things that grow have no owners.

He went looking for a firm mountaintop to plant it, and when he found the picnic can perfect territory, the botanist declared that was also this

Exactly a million years ago, a botanist found a bamboo seed and decided it was his.

As soon as a seedling sprouted, the botanist told it "you belong to me" and the seedling did its best to try and understand these words

Every new culm the sapling grew the botanist tickled declared his. And when the sapling big the new shoots, and those shoots new watchful leaves the botanist also claimed them.

When he started his journey, the entire clearing which was now a bamboo forest walked, then ran with him. Feeling as though he wasn't moving, the botanist tried to prune his way out.

One exerted day the botanist truth heard
of a second botanist who existed somewhere
far, and considered the possibility
of never being glacial lonely again.

And we let him.
We let him try.

gardening
mischief
grow
seedling
leaf
try
feeling
claim
understand
hear
clearing
feeling
new
forest
seedling
moving
understand
possibility
far
patience
sprout
botanist
rhythm
decide
boat
grow
sprout

FLUSH=HERB
GRAB=BLURB=BAG
ENTHUSIASM=MOB=BOSS=BLURB=BAG=GLIB=BESIDES=SAPLING
HERB=BARS=SHADOW=WATCHFUL
ENTHUSIASM=MOB=BOSS=SHADOW=WALK
DILEMMA=ATTAIN=NO=OBVIOUS=SEEDLING
DIG=GRAB=BEGINNING=GOAL=LET
EASE=EXPEDITE=EDGE=EXCHANGE=ENTIRE=YET=TOP=PUBLIC=CUNNING
SEMI=INDEED=DWELL=LEND=DAY
TRACT=TOAD=DISC=CO=OASIS=SOON
CROP=PROVERB=BEAM=MOB=BLAST=THING
EXERCISE=ESTATE=ECO=OWNER
RUB=BACTERIA=ABSORB=BENEFIT=THING
CAMEO=OPTICS=SNOB=BACTERIA=AGO
CLUB=BELIEF=FEELING=GAG=GANG=GROW
JOB=BRING=GO=OBSESS=SUCCUMB=BAMBOO
CO=ORCA=AESTHETIC=CLUB=BOOT=THING
STIFF=FOREGO=OBSESS=STEER=RHYTHM

STATIC=CURB=BUT=THOUGHT=TICKLED
DOGMA=ABSORB=BEANS=SUCCUMB=BELONG
CLUB=BENEFITS=SILVER=RAJ=JOURNEY
DILEMMA=ATTAIN=NO=OBVIOUS=SEEDLING
DIG=PRIORI=INN=TOP=PUBLIC=CUNNING
INSOMNIA=APLOMB=BELLIGERENT=THING
GRAB=BLURB=BAG=GLIB=BESIDES=
STATIC=CURB=BUT=THOUGHT=TIC
BEGINNING=GOAL=LIMB=BOOKS=SI
VERB=BASIS=SHOW=WHAT=TRIP=P
WHAT=THOU=UNDERSTAND=DEVELOP
BULB=BEACH=HERB=BOOM=MISCH
SNUB=BENEFIT=TREND=DEAL=LO
CLING=GRAB=BEGINNING=GOAL=LET
DOGMA=ABSORB=BEANS=SUCCUMB=BELONG
THROW=WILD=DNA=ALLOW=WHAT=T

Gardening is a relationship of patience. And faith.

Things that grow have their own rhythm.

Things that grow have no owner.

Exactly a million years ago, a botanist found a bamboo seed and decided it was his.

He went looking for a firm mountaintop place to plant it, and when he found the thickest compost-rich territory, the botanist declared that was also his.

As soon as a seedling sprouted, the botanist told it "you belong to me" and the seedling did his best to try and understand those words.

Every new dawn the sapling grew, the botanist trickled declared his. And then the sapling big gave new shoots, and those shoots new watchful leaves, the botanist also claimed them.

One exerted day the botanist truly heard of a second botanist who existed somewhere far, and considered the possibility of never being glacial lonely again.

When he started his journey, the entire clearing which was now a bamboo forest, walked, then ran with him. Feeling as though he wasn't moving, the botanist tried to prune his way out.

And we let him sprout. We let him try.

Floating words: let · try · grow · mischief · boat · gardening · understand · decide · free · claim · journey · seedling · relationship · rhythm · gardening · forest · far · moving · feeling · possibility · hear · leaf · botanist · clearing · new · grow · sprout · patience · possibility

---

Vertical word-chains (read top to bottom):

```
TAND=DEVELOP=PRUNE
EGINNING=GOAL=LET
DIG=GRAB=BEGINNING=GOAL=PRUNE
EASE=EDGE=EXPEDITE=EBB=BRIEF=FOREST
ENTHUSIASM=MOB=BOSS=SHADOW=WALK
VERB=BASIS=SHOW=WHAT=TRIP=PATIENCE
BULB=BEACH=LIMB=BOOM=MISCHIEF=FAITH
BEGINNING=GOAL=ALLOW=WHAT=THING
HROW=WILD=DNA=ALLOW=WHAT=THING
ABSORB=BENEFIT=THING
PRIORI=INNUENDO=OBJECTIVE=EXISTED
TRACT=TOAD=DISC=CO=OASIS=SOON
SILVER=RAJ=JOURNEY
EAM=MOB=BLAST=THING
BELIEF=GRIEF=FAITH
TJ=JOB=BELIEF
YET=TOP=PUBLIC=CUNNING=GLACIAL
SEMI=INDEED=DWELL=WATCHFUL=DAY
EXERCISE=ESTATE=ECO=OWNER
FLUSH=HERBARS=SHADOW
DOGMA=ABSORB=BEANS=BACTERIA=AGO
AESTHETIC=CLUB=BOOT=THING
SNUB=BENEFIT=TREND=DEAL=LONG
CLUB=BELIEF=FEELING=GAG=GANG=GROW
CAMEO=OPTICS=SNOB=EXCHANGE=ENTIRE
EASE=EXPEDITE=EDGE=BUT=THOUGHT=TICKLED
MA=ATTAIN=NO=OBVIOUS=SEEDLING
STATIC=CURB=BUT=THOUGHT=TICKLED
BLURB=BAG=GLIB=BESIDES=SAPLING
INSOMNIA=APLOMB=BELLIGERENT=THING
STIFF=FOREGO=OBSESS=STEER=RHYTHM
ING=GO=OBSESS=SUCCUMB=BAMBOO
```

Gardening is a relationship of patience. And faith.

Things that grow have their own rhythm.

Things that grow have no owners.

Exactly a million years ago, a botanist found a bamboo seed and decided it was his.

He went looking for a firm mountaintop place to plant it, and when he found the picnic camp perfect terriAcoy, the botanist declared that was also his.

As soon as the seedling sprouted, the botanist told it "you belong to me" and the seedling did its best to try and understand those words.

Every new calm the sapling grew, the botanist tickled declared his. And when the sapling big gave new shoots and those shoots new watchful leaves, the botanist also claimed them.

One exerted day the botanist truth heard of a second botanist who existed somewhere so far, and considered the possibility of never being glacial lonely again.

When he started his journey, the entire clearing which was new a bamboo forest, walked, then ran with him. Feeling as though he wasn't moving, the botanist tried to prune his way out.

And we let him.

We let him try.

Vertical word-chains:

BEGINNING=GOAL=LIMB=BOOKS=START

EASE=EDGE=EXPEDITE=EBB

SNUB=BENEFIT=TREND=DEAL=LONELY

LURB=BAG=GLIB=BESIDES=SAPLING

WHAT=THOU=UNDERSTAND=DEVELOP=PRUNE

DILEMMA=ATTAIN=NO OBVIOUS=SEEDLING

BULB=BEACH=HERB=BOOM=MISCHIEF=FAITH

CAMEO=OPTICS=SNOB=BACTERIA=AGO

CLING=GRAB=BEGINNING=GOAL=LET

VERB=BASIS=SHOW=WHAT=TRIP=DISC=OASIS=SOON

HROW=WILD=DNA=ALLOW=WHAT=THING

INSOMNIA=APLOMB=BELLIGERENT=THING

YET=TOP=PUBLIC=CUNNING=GLACIAL

SEMI=INDEED=DWELL=LEND=DAY

ENTHUSIASM=MOB=BOSS=SHADOW=WALK

CROP=PROVERB=BEAM=MOB=BLAST=THING

CLUB=BENEFITS=SILVER=RAY=JOURNEY

RUB=BACTERIA=ABSORB=BENEFIT=THING

STATIC=CURB=BUT=THOUGH=TICKLED

EXERCISE=ESTATE=ECO OWNER

OREGO=OBSESS=STEER=RHYTHM

FLUSH=HERB=BARS=SHADOW=WATCHFUL

DOGMA=ABSORB=BEANS=SUCCUMB=BELONG

O=OBSESS=SUCCUMB=BAMBOO

PRIORI=INNUENDO=OBJECTIVE=EXISTED

CO=ORCA=AESTHETIC=CLUB=BOOT=THING

CLUB=BELIEF=FEELING=GAG=GANG=GROW

DIG=GRAB=BEGINNING=GOAL=LET

EASE=EXPEDITE=EDGE=EXCHANGE=ENTIRE

Scattered words:

claim · try · free · hear · decide · grow · gardening · let · journey · gardening · mischief · boat · moving · botanist · understand · possibility · relationship · seedling · patience · far · feeling · forest · new · leaf · sprout · possibility · rhythm · clearing

VI. Ivy Roots

ivy   hardly

would   move

outside

Human walked past seedlings outside.

ivy   grow   become
        plants   naturally   self

        may

Human may not have even noticed.

ivy   pale   leather   unionism

grows   brown   collar

Human dropped   phone

something while

talking on the phone.

ivy   right   away   some   keeping   mind   god
      looked   arm   or   difficulty   open   whether
         conversation

Human had a conversation.

ivy   better   existing   using   languages
      thought   conditions   data   several

         intuition

Human had an intuition.

ivy   wish   will   where   if   favorite   should
      may   fulfillment   learn   else   my   meal

         daydream

Human had a daydream.

ivy   emphasis   my   formed   consequences   reasonably
      growing   away   lips   its   might
      language

Human had a language.

ivy   will   children   abroad   treatment   adopted
      plants   help   living   during   methods

         lover

Human had a lover.

human   can   control   contain   parts

hand   take   should   five

followed

And ivy followed.

human   would   your   should   really   ever   help

qualities   cause   mother   never   ought   need

root

Ivy stretched roots accross wall.

not
possibly
  can
 ground
 level
 every
  loved
           ivy

throughout
recognized
immediately
  went
  ever
  nothing
  loved

       ivy

            away
           nights
           summer
           every
            loved

              ivy

        ivy

  loved
   thee
 alone
would   ivy
feel

    loved
    ones
    left
   some
  patients
 undergoing
  great

Ivy loved.

      ivy

   loved
   god
  created
   his

   room

      ivy

       loved
  ivy   books
            would
             therefore
               can
  loved   best
   every   advantage
     reader
      not
       until

human could his before serious
condition carry mind becoming
speed

Ivy noticed speed.

human clashes change live my their out
personality may could without back money
light

Ivy noticed light.

human will out mind put should anything
souls find my could everything expect
metal

Ivy noticed metal.

human near wrath no can ball interest
habitation cape will children play bearing
warmth

Ivy noticed warmth.

human inflows distances self still leaves
capital equal greater can fresh before
seed

Ivy noticed seeds.

ivy walked
cottage
Human walked. street
names
being
lost

ivy lost
vines
may
Human got lost. give
effect
until

ivy until
plant
products
Human walked and got lost until... include
your
room

ivy room
vine
will
feel
Human walked and got lost until... your room, able
or

ivy or
day
long
Human walked and got lost until... your room, or line
up
here

Human walked and got lost until... your room, or her

food
bring
will
purpose
its
against
together
met
needs
librarian
reference
without
ideas
different
show
texts
printed
edition
peters
ivy

here

VII. Wander

delightful
weird
impossible
wet
vague
pleasant
nice
frightful
vivid
fond
faithful

A faithful handful
dream
of dreams

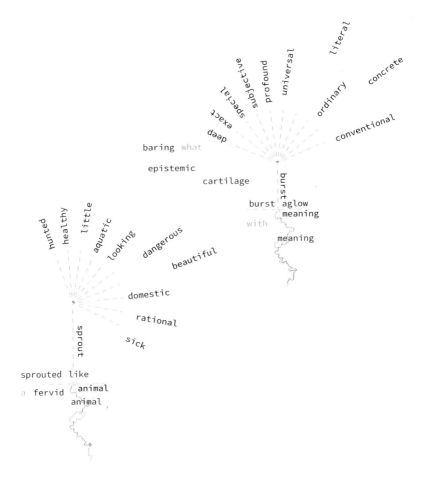

literal

special
subjective
profound
universal
exact
ordinary
deep
concrete

baring what
conventional

epistemic

cartilage
burst

burst aglow
with meaning

meaning

hunted
healthy
little
aquatic
looking
dangerous
beautiful

domestic

rational

sprout
sick

sprouted like
a fervid animal
animal

under

pleasant   will   waiting   ranging

places   still   periods

Impossible impossible   system

but   pleasant :

dangerous and beautiful   containing

we followed   or   side

beautiful   can   each

gardens give   period   chains

social   his

the   social temperature of orchids

orchid   outside

meeting

club

border   places

accross literal concrete

itself

and condescending   borders

S — PLATING
K — SKATING
EXCRUCIATING
ERATING
EXHILARATING
ACCOMMODATING
MATING
CAPTIVATING
waiting

EMBRACE
TRACE
GRACE
DISGRACE
LACE
SPACE
BRACE
EFFACE
place

(places will still waiting periods.

CARDIN
GARDEN
SARDAN
CARDEN
BARDEN
DARDEN
TEAGARDEN
CHARDIN
garden

Gardens can give each

CHUBB
BUB
SQUIB
DUB
SNUB
SUB
DRUB
GRUB
club

SNIDE
DECIDE
BACKSLIDE
RESIDE
SLIDE
ASIDE
COINCIDE
EYED
outside

club meeting places outside itself   ).

alt   tee   cue
aunt   thee   cage
abe   audit   twice   cache
able   arrest   twelve   clause
arise   atheist   tensile   culture
averse   arrogant   tangible   concrete
animate   anarchist   tolerance   clearance
advocate   assessment   turbulence   chromosome
alongside   arrangement   townspeople   consecutive
accumulate   astonishment   testosterone   circumstance
acupuncture
acquiescence

adrift   trace   coincide

aside

grub   grace

Yet   aside   adrift   traces coincide

anchoring

anchoring grub and grace to space space

aunt

turbulence

arise

chromosome

thee

clause

concrete

accumulate

cue

animate

twelve

tangible

anarchist

wilderness

searching

alone

polar
around
woods
grounds
far
path
pole

wander

off

ghost

mistake
find   random
desert
worlds
planet
drift
streets
looking

wander

So we wander off.
off

```
S       W       W
K       A       O               W
I       T       R               O
=       E       D               L
I       R       =               F
N       =       D               =
T       R       I               F
E       I       S               I
R       B       C               R
F       =       E               M
A       B       R               =
C       O       N               M
E       O       I               O
=       K       N               B
E       S       G               =
T       =       =               B
H       S       G               E
E       T       R               G
R       A       I               I
E       T       E               N
A       I       F               N
L       C       =               I
=       =       F               N
L       C       E               G
O       A       W               =
O       M       =               G
P       P       W               H
=       =       O               O
P       P       R               S
A       A       L               T
T       T       D
H       H
```
Through paths in worlds of ghosts,
        polar wood   searching street

and polar woods, and searching streets,

        looking for more planet nests

                like this.

```
                    /daylight
              clock|day
                    /clock
              alone|time
                alone\
                 only|eighths
              one-eighth\
              eighth|book
                        b
                        o
                        o
                        k
    There's grief in books
                        beginning

but there are beginnings
```

and alone time to fill flesh with words

so that forests

bit
solution   searching
sequence   dynamic
simulation
                constant
sort
                element
values

algorithm

time

hid
hand
hated
heated
hearted
homeland
humankind
heightened
highlighted
hypothesized

hold

breath

C F P B W W
H U E I O O
I R R R O R
L T T T L T
D H H H W H
B   O
I   R
R   T
T   H
H

earth

sal
sell
skill
samuel
spatial
skillful
sectional
successful
sacrificial
supplemental

sea

S U B M U M F A
C N E A P O H O
H E H N O H U L
O F M Z O U L D
O O O E L L F
L L D D D O D
    D   L D
          D

hold

inheritable\
familial|bicornuate
        /bicornuate
rudimentary|uterus
rudimentary\
underlying|lawsuit
        /action at law
ethical|action
    ethical\
moral|precept
        /precept
applicable|principle
applicable\
practical|workaday
    workaday\
everyday|talk

talk

lung

can

A
M
O
N
G
=
G
R
A
B
=
B
O
I
S
T
E
R
O
U
S
=
S
H
O
A
L

gathering

T S I C S S O P
H T N L W P F R
I R L I I R F I
N I I N N I S N
G N N G G N P G
  G G   G R
          I
          N
          G

sing

sue
some
seize
settle
suppose
sprinkle
supervise
suggestive
susceptible
significance
silence

wander

primitive
square
characteristic
thick
deepest
distal
yellow
arrow
deeper

bookshelf

std
sped
sword
stayed
spoiled
startled
strangled
sanctioned
synthesized
superimposed
seed
dream

root

/psychoanalysis
definitive|analysis
general-purpose\
general|proctor
        /proctor
regular|monitoring
    regular\
daily|reality
        /reality
altitudinous|world
altitudinous\
high|lowest
        lowest\
        least|mitigated
counterbalanced\
balanced|ecosystem

ecosystem

flow

gathering   trespassing   reading   does   little

        sign   experience   my   thing

now

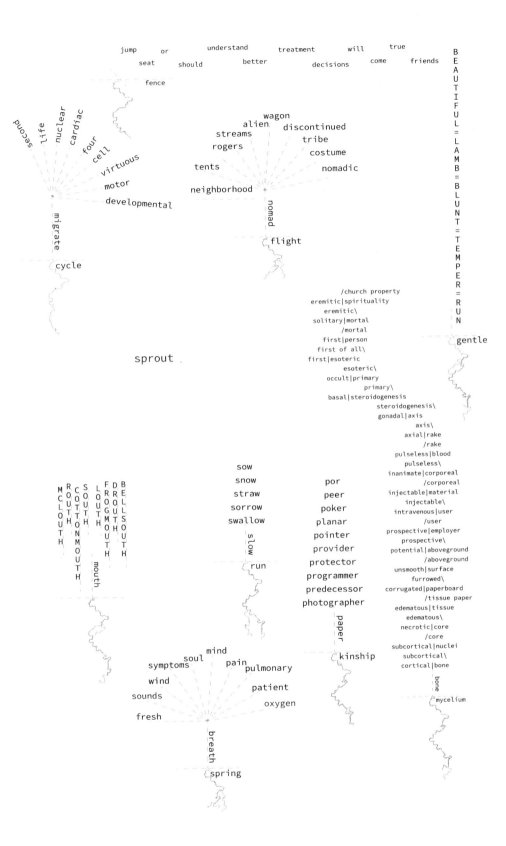

jump or understand treatment will true
seat should better decisions come friends

BEAUTIFUL=LAMB=BLUNT=TEMPER=RUN

fence

second life nuclear cardiac four cell virtuous motor developmental

wagon
alien discontinued
streams tribe
rogers costume
tents nomadic

neighborhood

nomad

migrate

flight

cycle

/church property
eremitic|spirituality
eremitic\
solitary|mortal
/mortal
first|person
first of all\
first|esoteric
esoteric\
occult|primary
primary\
basal|steroidogenesis
steroidogenesis\
gonadal|axis
axis\
axial|rake
/rake
pulseless|blood
pulseless\
inanimate|corporeal
/corporeal
injectable|material
injectable\
intravenous|user
/user
prospective|employer
prospective\
potential|aboveground
/aboveground
unsmooth|surface
furrowed\
corrugated|paperboard
/tissue paper
edematous|tissue
edematous\
necrotic|core
/core
subcortical|nuclei
subcortical\
cortical|bone

gentle

sprout

sow por
snow peer
straw poker
sorrow planar
swallow pointer
provider
slow protector
run programmer
predecessor
photographer

MCLOUTH ROUTHCOTTONMOUTH SOUTH FLOUTHFROGMOUTH DROUTH BELLSOUTH

mouth

paper

kinship

bone

mycelium

mind
soul pain
symptoms pulmonary
wind patient
sounds oxygen
fresh

breath

spring

Appx. Illustrated Field Guide

All the seedlings_ have a shared structure of a seed word and a domain word. The seed is the starting point of the wandering journey of the language while the domain word limits the wandering within a certain topic, so that the generated content won't be too dispersed. Plants can also have roots, which grow downwards. If the tip reaches a soil word, it will pick this word up as the new domain word and regrow the plant using this new domain.

```
                    private\
          personal|distress
                  /distress
            more|trouble
             more\
       less|syrupy
             syrupy\
          sweet|entreaty
                /entreaty
       solitary|prayer
          solitary\
     single|minute
              minute\
           second|subsection
                 /subsection
            last|paragraph
              last\
          final|solution
                /solution
          soft|answer

                 s
                 o
                 f
                 t

                  word
```

A Plant takes the seed that needs to be either a noun or an adjective, and tries to find the corresponding adjective/noun pair of the given word. For example, if the seed is "soft," then a potential noun that can be described by "soft" is "answer." Then the algorithm attempts to diverge a bit from the next word by finding another word that has similar meaning. The Plants grow from the tension between pairing and diverging.

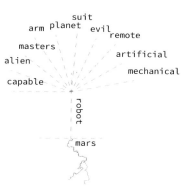

Dandelion asks the Datamuse server for trigger words that are statistically associated with the query word in the same piece of text. They are words that might appear in the same article with the seed word in the given domain.

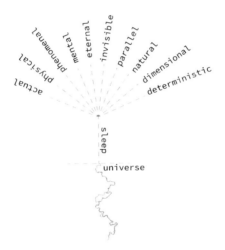

actual
physical
phenomenal
mental
eternal
invisible
parallel
natural
dimensional
deterministic

sleep

universe

Ginkgo shares certain visual similarities with Dandelion, but the inner logic of the generated words is quite different. It finds adjectives that are often used to describe the domain word. The goal is to introduce unexpected adjectives to associate with the seed word.

F
E
E
L
I
N
G
=
G
O
=
O
N
O
M
A
T
O
P
O
E
I
A
=
A
L
G
O
R
I
T
H
M

love

In Bamboo, words are displayed vertically. It takes the first letter of the seed word and searches for the next word in context that ends with the same letter. It iterates this process until the Bamboo reaches pre-defined height limit or grows out of the canvas.

void   because   men   find   society
        contract   those   shall   information

    internet

Ivy grows word by word by finding a potential frequent follower of the given word. If a seed word is "I", then a potential frequent follower would be "am". The sequence could reach to an end if a punctuation mark is generated or if the sequence is getting too long. Since the next word is only determined by the previous word, the overall context of the sentence is ignored and what comes out of Ivy might not be grammatically correct as a sentence.

```
               emg
              ewing
             easing
            ensuing
           entering
          excepting
         exhibiting
        encouraging
       encountering
               ending
               day
```

Pine is composed of a set of words in the provided context, which start and end with the same letters as the seed word. The width of each word decreases gradually as it reach the tip of the Pine, where a word with the shortest length of three letters tends to be found.

Willows are sensitive to sound and grow words that rhyme with the given seed vertically from top to bottom. Unlike other seedlings_, it can also grow without a given domain. This is because rhymes limit the potential words to be grown more than other rules and could have too few results if it is further constrained by a domain.